HUGH MCMILLAN is a poet fror
way. He has written five full c
at events and poetry festivals w
from the Hedge was a winner   ....
in 2009, a prize he won again for *Sheepenned* in 2017; as part
of that prize, he became Michael Marks Poet in Residence for
the Harvard Summer School in Napflio, Greece. He was also a
winner of the Smith Doorstep Poetry Prize and the Cardiff Inter-
national Poetry Competition. *Devorgilla's Bridge* was shortlisted
for the Michael Marks Award and in 2015 was shortlisted for
the Basil Bunting Poetry Award. In 2014 Hugh was awarded the
first literature commission by the Wigtown Book Festival to cre-
ate a work inspired by John Mactaggart's *The Scottish Gallovid-
ian Encyclopaedia* (1824); *McMillan's Galloway* was published
in limited edition in 2015 and in a revised edition from Luath
in 2016. His selected poems *Not Actually Being in Dumfries*
were published by Luath Press in 2015 and this was followed by
Heliopolis and *The Conversation of Sheep* by Luath in 2018 and
Haphazardly in the Starless Night and *Whit If?* in 2021. He has
featured in many anthologies, and three times in the Scottish Po-
etry Library's online selection *Best Scottish Poems of the year*. His
poems have also been chosen three times to feature on National
Poetry Day postcards, the latest in 2016. In 2020 he was chosen
by the Scottish Poetry Library as one of four 'Poetry Champions'
for Scotland, to seek out and commission new work, and was
given the role as editor of *Best Scottish Poems 2021*.

Split

LAN

:ed

996

a Press, 2009
, 2010

, 2012
ed, 2015
th Press, 2015
ide by an Unreliable

ess, 2018
uath Press, 2021
h, Roncadora Press, 2022
2023
t hiv bin, Luath Press, 2021;

First published 2024

ISBN: 978-1-80425-140-9

The paper used in this book is recyclable. It is made from low-chlorine pulps produced in a low-energy, low-emission manner from renewable forests.

FSC
www.fsc.org
FSC C022387
The mark of responsible forestry

Printed and bound by
Robertson Printers, Forfar

Typeset in 10.5 point Sabon by
Main Point Books, Edinburgh

Andrew, Lydia and Jasmine,
my wonderful talented trio

Contents

Part 1

Glass

Hole in the Sky

A half-empty train and
the north of England flicking
by in deep shades of green
and wild hawthorn.

I am sipping wine
and you are carefully judging
the smoothie you drink.
Food is a map we spread

out and navigate by:
we sometimes get lost there.
The sun is on your face, you
are smiling, but I have never

been more scared.
Can we make this day
a paradigm? One to fall
back on through the clouds.

Glass

The cold seeps
through the windows
of Whitby.
The sea is wild
and beautiful
today, you say,

it is shattering
on the walls
and moles and jetties.
At night the strings
of bulbs are twisted
over and over

by the fingers
of the wind.
While you sleep
I walk
the long pier.
Each bench bears

a story and
they jut into
the gleaming heart
of the ocean,
the young, the old,
the taken.

Later you shop
for jet but you
are glass
coming down
the steps, light
is through you.

Picture

Because she is a treasure
years in making,
I picture her in her white dress,
her floral top, her fringe,
a palm cupped
to shade her eyes from
the sun.

That picture
must ward off harm
in this world of complex cruelty.
She said she doesn't want
to live, it hurts too much,
and since then
I have been

writing about that picture,
wherever there is a blank page
or a space full of fear,
it is that picture I would show:
I would have it in every pocket,
that rocket to Mars,
I would print a million,

one for every lamp-post
and dashboard, and fan them
across the earth
so you could see what I mean.
The skirt, the top,
the fringe, the hand trying to keep
back the light.

Miracle

The sun is here,
blinkering
the unwary eye.
Even now at the turn

of winter it makes
flowers into plates
of gold, pebbles to glass.
I am writing a small

tribute to someone
I love, it is right
every moment
should have its ceremony,

every blaze and flicker.
It takes a million
years for energy
to reach from the centre

of the sun
to the surface,
then 8.6 seconds
to come to us.

Imagine that,
walking through
ancient light into the wreckage
of another year.

The Walks

Every day I walk round
the fields past the bench
and the hut, over the gate
and through the avenue of trees
that groan in the wind.

All this year my daughter
has walked with me,
in that hand-me-down parka
with its enveloping furry hood.
Mostly I watch her trainers

moving over the ground.
She doesn't stumble but glides
above, she is so light. Her face
is pointed to the canopy
of branches, to the sun

breaking in. I know her face,
it is beautiful, but I suppose
our minds are closed to one
another, no matter how much
we love or want. I tell myself

these days are a blessing.
Here we are again, at this junction
of thorn and sap. One day she'll keep
on. She surely must, she will take
a road, and I will turn on my step.

Diverted to Split

Somewhere
in the unscarred
skies, in a fabulous
scaffold of blue

the way was parted,
some piece of muscle,
like thin fabric gave out
just like that, a wee,

very wee thing, like
life in fact. Imagine
lying streaked
with the sun on the shore,

draw me
a map of the Adriatic
from above,
in cloud white as bone.

Light is a dream
of breathlessness,
and only an inch
from sleep.

Something's Up

My face is hot today. The clouds
are hemming the sky but the centre
is an inflammable blue. I do not

want the world or myself to unzip
or the sky to fall in. I am scared
of clouds. Poets are not weather

vanes or especially important,
but it's no longer clear what words
to write, whether the lines will run.

I'm sorry but the afternoon
is too perfectly blue, a distant
plane makes a single fault line.

Not Right

I took the train advice to heart –
'Phone us if it doesn't look right' –
and said the man three rows down
didn't look right at all, he had the wrong
hat and the pub last night didn't look
right and was smelly too to be honest.
I'm on the train now and the view
out of the window does look right,
there are three trees on top of a hill
of bracken and a stream like a diamond
chain and two sheep running away
comically, but also there's my head
at the forefront. I have to tell you,
my head, it doesn't look right at all.

Yellow Horses

A friend leads me to
the Navajo legend of the horses,
how they were corralled
into the four corners of the world,
white horses to the east,
turquoise horses to the south,
yellow horses to the west,
and spotted horses to the north,
the colours of the compass,

the colours of morning, noon,
afternoon, and night.
She writes that her granddaughter
arrived on an abalone horse
in the early winter morning.
I'm standing here below
trees which stretch like fingers
at the end of a day in this bit
of Scotland and I start crying – oh yes,

it is because of my own problems,
but let us not discount the miracle
of that birth across the ocean, and the horses too,
in my head like the horses my daughters
rode when they were young.
We are all touched by the same sky,
the same misery and joys,
the coming and goings; it all happens under
the same shell-coloured sky.

PART II

Rose

Spring 2022

The birds never sing at Auschwitz,
but they do.
Poppies burst through
dead men's chests,

all kinds of flowers bloom
in broken walls, in the gaps
where schools once stood.
Plants and weeds and birds

don't count how many books
they're in, are immune
to their symbolic place.
I don't even think they wish,

as I would in their shoes,
that we'd fuck off: they just
don't care. The birds never
sing at Auschwitz, but they do.

Nina Demchak

Among all the horrors, I am drawn
to Nina Demchak who is carrying

her arthritic dog for three days
to Poland because he 'simply

couldn't be left behind.'
I have responsibilities too,

but not a personnel carrier
burning outside my house.

We keep these stories close
because we imagine the indomitably

human will overcome brute force,
that the diamonds found

will last longer than the dust,
but we have been pressing

Ninas, these precious
fragments, onto the hem of history

for a thousand years and sick
old men are still centre stage.

The Gap

*'There's a gap between
the promise and its
fulfilment on the ground'*
Anthony Blinken

In the gap,
more a chasm or vacuum,
people live and die,
water is poisoned
by body parts,
children rot in incubators.

In the gap, tomorrow
is a dream, or ongoing
nightmare.
The gap is what follows
speeches, in the place of
incredulity and rage.

The gap is what we fill
with wine and Christmas,
or lines of poetry
that shuffle along the page
like old soldiers dimly
remembering parade.

Anchorage

Anchorage, the haven
at the end of the ocean,
where old sailors spat and yarned
while nature hemmed them in:
the Anchorage of my imagination.

The fact is though,
Anchorage like any other town
at the edge of nowhere,
is an oil slick in a crystal sea,
where hungry beasts and men

rake through bins.
It's no consolation
to the planet we have wrecked
to write poetry, but my mind
is in retreat and so there will

always be an Anchorage,
where the storm
is thwarted and in some cabin
hope and love splutter like flame.
The world we have dreamed,

is not the world we dream of.
There is no relation at all.
God speed my children
on their voyages
across the frost.

The Girls in the Wood

There's a mob of small girls
who roam the woods here.
You can hear distant calls
like birds or monkeys,
but it is rare to see them.

Folk who do are eager to pass
the knowledge on – almost
in hushed tones they say,
'yes, we maybe spied them under
a bridge wading in green water,'

or, 'I'm sure I caught a glimpse
by the old deer hide,
they were wearing red wellingtons.'
I think it is the mob of small girls
in the wood who built that shelter

made of intricately laced branches,
hazel twisted into ribs and logs
inside for tiny seats.
They are never there when I pass,
though often there is a slight

stir as if the place has just
emptied and I imagine
in the shadows between trees,
those leaves wet with rain,
are eyes gleaming.

Whatever it is about the mob
of small girls in the wood,
they are not faeries or ghosts,
though sometimes
when I hear cries lost in the wind

I let myself feel they are.
That is ridiculous: in the village
these girls are well known.
But in the woods!
When people talk of it,

the smeddum, the indivisibility,
it takes them back.
Even the hardest of them,
who have lost the most,
it takes them back.

The Chair

Granite and lichen,
scuffed grass
and water stretching
to the hills where clouds
hang like steam.

I have taken this
view into my heart:
though old as the ice age,
it is home,
the people clinging to its sides,

the sea birds skimming water,
the snort of the sea,
the far-off bell sounding
for those trying still
to make sense of it.

It is good because
there is no end and beginning,
no sentiment.
It is just wind on the face
and rain to come.

Glasgow Epiphany

In the station buffet
are two teenagers
too old for juice but too
young for public alcohol so
they are drinking Monster.

The girl has long, dark hair
and a grey cap and is
sobbing uncontrollably
for short periods
of time, though she

is laughing and smiling too –
sometimes the laughing
smiling and sobbing
uncontrollably
merge into a noise

almost like a song.
Throughout this, the boy,
who has a black coat
and holly berry earrings,
talks in a quirky monotone,

only gently increasing
his voice during the most
uncontrollable
sobbing so that she might
better hear.

It is clear he has nothing
to do with the upset –
they are friends who have met
Christmas shopping
and are now here

in the corner of the buffet
talking in this heightened
and exultant way.
A few folk glare at him
but they have not been

following: they are not in tune.
He is glancing at the clock,
not from boredom
or embarrassment
but because he doesn't want

any train to come,
or any afternoon like this
to end. He knows that
at the very apex
of this uncontrollable

sobbing and laughter,
he is the one
to whom she is turning
her damp
and miraculous face.

Just Another Bog-Standard Sea Poem

A man with a ponytail
is telling me how sick my country is.
I reply countries are spits
of rock filled with shifting crowds
of morons. This satisfies him,
he is Dutch. Earlier he said
he is not allowed beer because
it makes him into a sadist
and I told him I am not allowed
beer because of that rash on my leg.
This was a good start
to our relationship, which has since
settled into a contented silence.
The light turns the sea
into a million fractured
pieces of spinning glass.

The Vibe at Stewarton

This has happened before.
Somewhere between Stewarton
and Kilmaurs, that roar
of the train, the open windows,

the relentless light,
the young folk screaming
and hopping about like birds,
and, suddenly, bliss,

a combination, I guess,
of a second plastic
bottle of Puglia Rosso
and a blast of air from

the Ayrshire Levant,
carrying perfumes
from camel trains and a hint
of the sea. Such warmth

and love I have now
for those who share my life,
but also these strangers,
that boy strangling

another with an over-long
woollen scarf,
and that orange nymph
dancing on a tabletop.

Workshop in a Highland School

When I arrive, the ceilidh band
is in full swing. I have eight
pupils fired up by poetry
as an alternative to Maths.

'You can embrace Maths
when the time comes,'
cries the teacher. 'That time
never will,' a child responds.

Each is given a cup
of hot chocolate and a piece
of blank paper. The workshop
is carefully constructed,

completely ignored. One girl
writes a poem about an anchovy,
another about things she's
never done, fighting a shark,

squaring a circle.
A boy writes a funny story
about how his mother
thinks the football highlights

are the whole game –
'She thinks it's so exciting,
I don't like to tell her.'
A girl recently arrived

from Cornwall describes
running round the streets
with her friends, and starts
to cry. I leave, my head

buzzing with poetry
and the mad,
sad power of children.
Outside, the sweet

sounds of a fiddle,
the water gleaming,
three kids still hiding
behind a bench from Maths.

Marys

My mother's kin
were all called Mary.
Census after census
shows houses filled

with Marys,
Elspeth now and then,
and grandweans,
(one called Mary),

but no men to be seen:
maybe they had gone
to war, to keep a lighthouse,
or were dead,

they were powerless
before the tide of history,
and the tide of Marys.
Words only say

so much. In the oral
tradition, stories
are more vibrant.
My mother Mary,

aged 16,
at the cottage
door storming out
across the sea

to Glasgow,
her mother, Mary,
who'd seen it all,
saying, you'll be back.

Piecing it Together

I am sitting in a poorly lit room
when darkness falls, noiselessly,
impenetrably, only a tiny glow
now and then across the Sound.

There's a cupboard with some
copies of *The Scots Magazine*
and a pile of scuffed board games,
and suddenly I realise this is

all the cottages and small hotels
I stayed in with my folks,
having tea or toasted
teacakes as the wind tossed

seagulls high above our heads
and long-scrapped ferries
beat paths to wet islands,
all of us sitting at the edge

of the fractured, familiar sea
in improbable blazers and coats,
reading, playing Newmarket,
our faces blurred and grey.

Of course no shelf of books
or Scrabble can bring back
the lost or dead, return me to that
state of innocence and dread:

the most that one can say is,
look at me after all this time
at the edge of the ocean still,
piecing it together.

Mythos

Pines grow in
mist this morning.
Cloud has fallen to earth
and the sky is a skin
on a well of blue waiting
to burn. In an hour or two
the heat will hit us,

we will find ourselves
suddenly standing
in the unfurled morning
by a barely moving river,
the hills with collars of spill
like gold. Imagine such a land

and its stories.
The tale of how Eithne
or Taliesin rid the land
of snakes and square-heads.
Of how wolves
killed the last shooter
in the lounge bar

of the Buccleuch.
All we need for this
is love, freedom
and high fever.
In such weather
dreaming is simply
borrowing from tomorrow.

Dream

A wide expanse of grass,
a stream meandering between
tiny trees. It is Versailles
below a pearl white sky.

I know this because we are
dressed in paper ribbons
of the most flamboyant kind,
yellow, red, aquamarine.

We waft in a breeze laced
with hyacinth and jasmine.
How posh we must be
to pirouette here half asleep

like kings and queens. Here
you are, so I know the gardens
are given over to poets between
three and four in the morning.

Good day! Good night!
See how the brain gathers us all
and shakes us out
on random chessboard lawns.

Sex and St Bridgid

(After Salvador Dalí)

Let me climb this ladder of words
to the tower room, and gaze
on your face which is turned to a window
open on fields like a Book of Days.

You have eyes like green ink.
I cannot keep up with
your pen, it is dancing
at your heels like a spaniel.

All day you write so the lost
of the world may have a place
in the hearth of page. But at night
when the stars hang on the fret

of branches like the glint
of a dream, your skin is white,
your blood has cooled,
is diluted by moonlight.

Catherine of Siena

(Carved from wood: Burrell Collection)

Catherine, her hand
across her heart,
her robes girded
about her, 'a true bride
ransomed by the blood
of Christ,' starved

herself to death at 33.
Look behind: they have
swaddled this woman then
cored her out. Impaled
her on a rude post.
The genius in one so young

and its only conduit
in the company of freaks
and madmen, or sleepless
nights lurid with dreams.
Such sanctity and passion.
Emptiness and waste.

The Death of Homer

Full moon, the trees are flags
or bunting flapping
like ghosts. These white
houses and the roads
that cross our lives,
the half-remembered
narratives.

Did he one day realise,
walking blind in the heat,
the sea a single blinding
sheet of light,
that the stones
in his hands were
balls of dirt?

He is spinning between
the ocean and the sky:
Hector stares from
the Skaian Gates,
Circe from her web of stars,
the man who made the world
is dead, in the mud of Ios.

The Scythian Women

Of the hundred Scythian
women sent to fight for
Alexander the Great before
the great battle of Jaxartes

twenty were interrupted
by their babies crying.
Hard to their task
said the historian,

they pierced
them with lances till
they were still, but
they didn't, they sang

them a quiet song about
the rivers of Taurus
till they fell asleep.
Of the hundred Scythian

women sent to fight for
Alexander the Great before
the great battle of Jaxartes
twenty met the Sarmatians

and at sword point
failed to cut their throats
till the blood ran like
ribbons of red

but instead formed
common cause
irrigated the steppes
with flowers like stars.

Of the hundred Scythian
women sent to fight for
Alexander the Great before
the great battle of Jaxartes

thirty stopped at
a blue lochan
below Eridanus
the celestial river

and did not engage
in rigorous
athletic competition
but lifted their

kilts above their
brown thighs
and made love.
Of the hundred Scythian

women sent to fight for
Alexander the Great before
the great battle of Jaxartes
twenty saw roads

leading like
arrows east
and west and their hearts
didn't fail

but swelled
with hope and
prospects and they turned
the bridles of their beautiful

horses towards the dawn.
Of the hundred Scythian
women sent to fight for
Alexander the Great before

the great battle of Jaxartes
ten remembered
their comrades
asleep, gone,

splayed, haloed
with light,
lifted their shields
and axes and charged,

their cries
not reminiscent
of vixens at all,
but wolves.

Rose

*(The rent for the tolls of the Auld Brig in Dumfries
was paid by the Minorite Friars to their Douglas
overlords in the shape of a fresh rose twice yearly.)*

A single rose was given
on the Auld Brig as rent
for the holy ground
east of the Nith,

the leper houses,
the cells, the cloisters.
One at Lammas,
one at Martinmas.

The Douglases knew
Christ's blood, they spilled
it often enough, built churches
on the bones of the dead.

The rent was paid between
earth and water, between
orchards and the midden
pits of Maxwelltown.

A flower was the price
if you were holy enough
to walk in the footsteps
of saints, the rest paid coin

or hauled themselves,
drenched and breathless,
across the Stake Ford.
The world was savage,

yet blooms were steps
to heaven, hell or fairyland.
Maybe still. Petals are bright
as wounds or doors.

St Michael's

Water blackens stones,
stains like ink spots seeping through,
bursting in moss like puss.

Time has rid us of names
apart from the carefully chiselled.
'The Friends of Robert Burns',

Dr Carmichael, Mrs Chisholm, etc,
the Burns Society remembers
them in little blue discs.

One served Burns beer,
talked behind his back,
another lent him five pounds,

dined out on it after his death.
'He wasna inclynt tae pey it eftir.'
Ministers still glower at their stone

flock, at the pauper's grave
where they flung Burns, weighed
down at last by small town misery

and spite. What a country to be born
and die in. And be resurrected,
of course, when it made commercial sense.

Keats in the Maxwell Arms, Dalbeattie

Do you see that pale boy
in the window with fierce eyes
and stars in his hair?
Behold, ye farmers

and long-distance lorry drivers,
ye posties and window cleaners,
ye jobless artisans,
behold the ghost of Keats!

Yes, you would probably
have broken a pool cue over
his head he was so weird,
aloof and racist.

Most folk thought he was
a thief or an army spy:
such is the lot of poets.
I'm sure, bathing

his wounds later,
you would have seen
his bandaged radiance,
a man like the rest of us

struggling with life
and burning for beauty,
just not that good
at mixing.

Makars

Solway has mist and cloud,
but sun will come,
and the channels
will light like fire.

The past is everywhere:
on this track, in this lost railway line,
in the boat's creak and slap
and timelessly here

too are the poets,
rifling their pockets
for words, some carefully,
some without care at all.

I guarantee I will meet
five poets today.
One will be having a meeting,
one will be submitting

to the *Tallahassee Review*,
one will be finessing
a poem about geese,
one will be sharing someone

else's poem about geese
on social media and saying
OMG this sums up geese
so completely I'm in awe,

and one will be naked,
channelling pain
and need with words
that tomorrow will be tarnished.

Ars Poetica

Poems are waiting to be written,
either strung out on a beach
at the ocean's edge or through
a train window calling like gulls.
They are on pier ends, rain-
soaked streets, in pub doorways.
They wade ashore, no end

of clamour. There are poems
that will never be written, circling
in a patch of ocean lit by the sun,
– but they are less trouble than the ones
that want to be. They squawk all night,
hop away on salt-webbed feet
just before you wring their necks.

Waterfoot

The ribs of the old jetty
and the throat
of the Solway
long and blue between
Seafield and Bowness.

The last view for many,
as the Firth gave way
to wide waters,
gave way to the world.
I am thinking how hard

it is to be a moment away
from love,
never mind a lifetime.
People did it. Wrote letters
on the whims of the waves,

sent cards and packets
opened under
dull or lurid skies.
Remembered,
I suppose, a particular

smile or sky or laugh,
and pinned it on a sleeve,
traced it with a finger
in the minutes
before dawn.

PART III

Joke

The Retirement of Len Lungo

It is a winter
afternoon in the Stag,
some pensioners are
watching the horses
on TV,

a drunk is losing
his shirt on the puggy,
the barman is
reading the *Daily Record*,
and two men are glued

together passionately kissing
where the huge
picture of Len Lungo
used to be.
Remember the one?

Him winning at
Cheltenham.
How times change:
he's not even working with
horses now.

The Dry Train

I am on a Dry Train – two old men
in high-vis jackets trudge up and down
the carriages and return with confiscated
bags of booze. Dire warnings are broadcast
regularly of the consequences of drinking
on this Very Dry Train: folk will be taken off
to the gaols and stockades of Kirkcaldy, even Inverkeithing.

As I write, more clank by: a dozen cans
of export and a bottle of Baileys.
This is a Dry Train, the Steward shrilly cries,
we are watching CCTV and can track
even vodka in coke bottles, we can see all this
from our complex command centre
on the Dry Train. Why, in a world

of unfettered misery, this is a Dry Train
is never explained. It is bad enough
travelling to England in the first place.
Maybe the train has been hijacked
by a mob of Presbyterians.
One thing is clear though:
of all trains everywhere, this is

the least dry. Everyone knows there is a carriage
up there groaning with contraband,
a cornucopia of malt and gin, real ale, Cointreau, cider,
Buckie, Pernod, cheap whisky, nail polish remover,
contact lens fluid, lighter fuel, a glittering mountain
of stimulants constantly added to,
constantly just out of reach.

Bitter Old Men

I'm on a shell of a bus rattling towards
Stranraer with two bitter old men
and a driver who is bitter too,
but not yet of pensionable age.
What has brought on this bitterness
on a morning pierced with daggers

of white sunlight like this is a mystery.
They are talking, sometimes to each other,
but mostly in a three-piece a cappella where
each addresses the universe from a tortured
place in their soul, and the bus, bitter too
at having lost its suspension near Crocketford,

joins in, wheezing a descant.
The young, who are not present,
are the main focus of their rage.
They have no manners or respect,
the young, they roam the streets
knocking old women into the paths

of vehicles. They leave cans of high-
energy drinks which, at every pothole,
crash up and down the bus like pebbles
on a bleak shore. Things were not like
this when these bitter old men were young,
though it is unclear when this was,

Dalmellington in the 18th century perhaps,
more likely never, for these men emerged
fully embittered and wizened as walnuts,
I am convinced, behind some wall

like that scene from *Terminator*.
I don't recognise the universe
these bitter old men represent although
their chanting is almost soothing,
like plainsong, and is it not near Christmas?
Remember, after the shepherds
came the bitter old men.
At Springholm two girls with ripped jeans

get on, loudly not at school – the men's
voices recede to whispers, they were not
expecting youth, they recoil as if before radiation.
Getting off at Castle Douglas, the girls stand aside
to let them by: 'age before beauty,' one says,
I'll say it before you have the chance.

Learning about the Religious Wars, Wigtown Book Festival 2022

I had to leave before the talk,
the streets were full of hooded
folk with green anoraks like monks
pacing in the rain between one book
and another, but in the pub

in Newton Stewart the barman
had just bought a huge crossbow
with a metal bolt in a car boot sale
and wanted to fire it 'to see what
happened.' I had just got a pint

of cider and looked on but thought,
even from my degree of ignorance,
that the complex winding mechanism
indicated no ordinary buy: indeed, it took
three men in Rangers tops some

minutes to load it. I imagine in warfare
one man in a Rangers top might be
trained to do this in half the time
using his 55 Nike Air Force trainers
as counter balance, but think of

the pressure as enemy horsemen
from the Holy Roman Empire bore down.
Even here, the barman had to stop
for a second to serve two sceptical girls
Baileys. Someone brought
a thick plank from the back to prop
against the wall and had

the presence of mind to draw the face
of a local Catholic friend upon it.
There was much laughter, whooping

and excitement and many folk
were told to stand back well out
of range. It was like Grunwald,
the mist of sweat, the breath,
the drum of anticipation like hoof beats,

the sun splintering through windows,
the puggy pulsing red as blood.
I was in the second line when
the fusillade fired, through the target,
two walls, a cupboard and a junction

box, lodging a few feet from a woman
watching *Homes Under the Hammer*.
She was reported to have exclaimed
'Hail Mary Mother of God,' thus settling
the conflict once and for all.

Archie's Bath Night
(From *The Druids – Bringing in the Mistletoe*
by EA Hornel and George Henry)

Here we are – Uncle
Archie on his annual
bath night, put out the flags.

They're spilling down
the hills under a full moon,
the Scallop sisters,

Archie's Samoan barber,
the neighbours,
that woman who does

the macramé, somebody
from the Airbnb
who thinks it's a festival,

three hippies –
Archie's got a hinging ee
for them.

Archie is 128 years
old and puts his longevity
down to filth.

Appreciating Botticelli's *Birth of Venus* after a Bad Piece of Fish

A naked girl glides eerily towards
the shore while two men throw up
and a waitress hurries to help
using a floral curtain she's ripped
from the toilet wall. It's a bad

seafood dream, like Titian's
*That Kebab Prometheus Ate Last
Night* where an eagle feasts on
raw entrails. Surprising, the extent
classical art was inspired by gastric

events: Holbein's *Getting Lifted
by the Polis* or Pieter van Noort's
A Night with the Paramedics
spring to mind. In the Italian school,
they enhance the effects with a sickly

palette: malachite, ultramarine,
whereas the Dutch like the drizzled
gloom of a Sunday night's drinking
on some Scottish strand, every ginnel
rife with grotesques or the glint of steel.

Óskópnir

There's a wake in the beer garden, weans fried
with juice, adults full of sunshine and gin.
The other hotel guests have gone inside,
they think it's bad form at such a time
to have a boom box, or be shouting fuck
through the lengthening vault of an afternoon.
You see death must be respected, sucked
up to, its threat and pomp not impugned,
its cremation plans fully up to date.
One should not be rolling upon the road
with both hands gripped around the neighbour's throat.
But the shadows are unloosed, darkness spreads!
Get in the Sourz, the Jägermeister bombs,
beat your voices like drums until the dawn!

Mourning

Let us leave this decrepit town
and join the throng of emaciated
citizens mourning the Queen.

On the long road south
we will read the nine best jokes
the Queen made and piss

ourselves. Let us remember
the pastel dresses she wore
while meeting arms manufacturers

and other psychopaths,
all done with that impish
twinkling eye her staff

swears blind she had. Be sure
to remember the exceptional
personal hardships she endured:

her husband dying in extreme
old age, and having to shell
out more than 12 million

quid to keep her boy out of clink.
What mother couldn't empathise?
And all the wars, 28

she signed off on,
imagine that. Of course,
just her name on the bottom

of the page,
it's not as if she represents
that flag and ruling class

who have shamed the world.
Poor woman can't be blamed
for that: great burden, the crown.

In heaven now I bet you:
a star has gone out forever,
etc, etc, etc, etc.

Old Joke

A dog walks into a bar and says
I can't see a thing, I'll open this one.
Archaeologists have unearthed
the first ever pub joke

but don't know what it means.
They have scooped out the inns,
re-brewed the beer,
uncovered menus daubed on walls,

found games and bar snacks.
They know what the average
labourer was paid and what in,
they know the endemic diseases,

droughts, famines, invasions,
the age their kids died at.
They have written books, PhDs,
documentary series,

podcasts for the Smithsonian.
They've been all over them with
a nit comb, but the Sumerians
still have the last laugh.

Kirkcudbright Graffiti

In the morning sunlight,
sprung on the masts of trawlers,
on the rooftops
of the ancient burgh,

its doocots, its sandstone,
its slate, let us dwell for a moment
on the tragic duality of Kyle Leitch,
doomed through eternity

to grass and shag deid folk.
Not to speak of Mags,
a perennial ride,
and the eponymous tragedy

of Dougie No Cock.
The walls are inked like
Giza. A tribe of bitter
priest-like folk have worked

for years here,
their crayons wearing down,
their candles burning to a wick,
cutting into the night

their spells and rituals.
Cursed is the cleaning fluid that
obliterates these voices
from this sacred space.

Zoom Poetry Reading

The poet has cropped hair
and reads of trees and misery.
Above, shelved like statuary,
are Luiz, Laura, Kate,

Evangeline, Siggi, Calum,
Rosa, Liz, and iPhone6,
their windows receding
miniatures in striped light.

Evangeline is pouring gin.
A black cat moves in a single
liquid moment across Rosa's lap.
The sun is breaking over

Calum like an egg,
iPhone6 is asleep, or dead,
her face turned like a spoon
towards the screen.

What brings them here,
their faces tenderly
hung like icons?
I'll just read several more:

an imperceptible rustling
like wind through shadows,
a stirring
in a dozen holy ponds.

Effie Macleod Is Not Available

In 1980 we set off
with our brand
new video cameras
to record the last
of the munitionettes.
One was taken ill immediately,

the next, Mrs Graves,
stoically received our tripod
in her pristine front room.
'I wis a hame-loving lassie,
steyed wi ma ma and dad
luwed the extra cash.

Met my late husband,
he was a polisman.'
This was not what we wanted,
Joyce and I, young hot-blooded
history teachers
on the hunt for tales

of drink and sexuality,
free girls making the most
of their freedom.
At last, after a custard
Cream, she conceded:
'Ah mind some frae Ireland,

worse, the islands, they
were wild as Rannoch,
they were aff their heids
the stuff they did –

drinking, hijacking trains,
playing fitba like men.
It was a national scandal
aw hushed up cos o the war.
Yon Effie Macleod wis
fae Raasay, spent mair
time in jankers than in the sheds.
She steys in Vancouver Avenue.

Ye ken whit the food train
brings her?
A bottle o vodka a day.
Hijacking trains!
Playing Fitba like men!
Jankers! Vodka!'

This was more like it.
We went to the pub,
drank beer, plotted
a visit to Effie: was this
the centre half of the legendary
Gretna Girls team

who hammered the Carlisle
Munitionettes at Brunton Park?
As we were packing
our equipment we heard news
that Mrs Graves had died –
a heart attack.

'There go the angels of death.'
joked the jannie as we left.
Our destination was a council house,
neat curtains, a ginger cat
on the step and a note on the door.
'Effie Macleod is no longer available for interviews'.

Colin Donati's Dinner

Two hours into the open mic,
I am coveting Colin Donati's dinner.
Being a real poet, he has spent the
evening in a fugue state,
his hunger was for another place,
the beams of his eyes were fixed
on the sublime, but there was a piece
of pie on his plate, or lasagne,
perhaps the last hard black bit.
I could imagine chips there
too in the shallow lagoon
below his Olympian gaze,
gravy maybe washing
on an unseen jagged shore.
Is it coincidence that the words
pastry and poetry are so similar?
I think not: they both speak of the soul,
so when the shadows deepen,
the words still rolling in relentless
tide, it is not just the food
that is fading from my sight,
it is the thin meal of happiness
gone, it is the crust
of kindness fading.

PART IV

Verge

Waiting Room

The bent ears of grass
ripple like water.
The sun is an infection:
starlings gleam,
brilliant petals hang

like cloud.
On a small chair
my bare knees sing with heat.
The day is in abeyance
as some days are:

a state of grace,
and here, a little summer.
The saint is opening
his wine
and my Greek girl

is moving bare-breasted
through white poppies.
Life is always beginning –
remember that
before you sleep.

Talking to Tony in the Stag

In the Café of Lost Youth
they have painted out
the nicotine but not completely.
Outside, the rain
has stopped beating on
old glass and the sun is risking it,
about to dash across the road.

The conversation...
Och, this is not some routine
poem about the dead
and the weight of years,
it is really about the light
and how it picks out each
leaf so the veins stand out

or takes every drop of water
in its palm to spin it, flickering
like a bright coin.
I know nothing today but this,
Tony. As long as there is light,
there will be a chance
of love.

The Lost

When you lose someone, what does it mean?
Are they mislaid? Has some small mistake
been made? Did they mean to meet
and talk about their news this week

but couldn't? That slight pause,
that's when they went beyond reach,
with their train tickets, their strange hats,
their parcels, their going to the shops.

They were lost in streets, pubs, buses,
at sea. Remember when my mother
was lost? I was at Loch Katrine.
walking in the cold and writing.

I called the waters blue as steel.
They were grey, probably.
That's where people get lost,
the gap between the blue and the grey.

A Fool on the Train

Fields combed with frost,
like grey bottle glass.
Fingers of trees
against the cold sky,
the sun daubed behind.

The man opposite
is singing, 'see me, I dinnae
give a fuck, your mammy
used to drive a truck.'
I'm not sure how

he knew that, about
my mammy and the truck.
She drove a two-ton
Bedford full of bombs
for Catalina flying boats,

more exciting, she said,
than being a maid.
Her war was sadness
and joy and opportunity,
I see that now, the time

she was most alive.
He moves down the carriage:
'Your father was the jannie
if you don't believe me
you're a fanny.'

A stir of recognition
down there, the plot
furthered in a rush
of scenery between
Stewarton and Kilmaurs.

On Earth

The schoolies
are leaving the bus,
all kicking plastic

bottles and laughing
for the sake of it
and I am left

with a couple
who are quietly raking
the embers.

She has bright
nails and a denim bag
firmly clasped

across her lap.
He has a semi serious beard
and a cap with a logo.

They go the hard miles
between Barbara Mill
and Closeburn,

studiously watching
verges flick by,
the iron of the railway,

the hills haunted
even in early summer.
Why she asks at last,

Why on earth?
The schoolies would
have made faces

at that, like clowns
through the empty glass
of the bus stop,

run home,
their laughter sharp
and mocking in the gloaming.

Why on earth?
I am drinking wine
and it seems to me

that as love streams
away it pools.
There is some humour

there, irony certainly.
The bus, the wine,
the schoolies, your faces

golden and broken
in the window. Listen,
love is everywhere.

The Pavement Outside the New Bazaar

I have never looked closely
at the pavement here
before, it is bright with
constellations. It is like
the night sky you see

lying on your back in Mull,
pregnant with stars.
A gull adds a new sun
as I watch, I am blessed.
Seabirds see the stones

scuffed by a hundred thousand
feet, like Robert Fergusson's,
his head full of death,
his pockets full of poems.
We string lights along

the edge of our lives
and hope they don't blink out.
Across the Nith, nursery kids'
high-vis jackets
glitter and are gone.

The Platform

A blurred line of hills and grey trees beyond
the roofs. Not the Acheron but Clyde.
There is a severe-looking man with a wet dog,
a woman with a limp and a boy carrying

a basketball whose face gleams with fine rain.
They are all here in the mist to share
this moment of comings and goings.
They have paused their intricate plans

to be here, walking so near they can swap
stories and dreams. Some are going
further who might have stayed, but honestly,
they have only passed into cloud, so close

they can be touched. And who leaves really,
when they have warmed like filaments so many
lives? The rails sing, they are lit to the end
of the world, from each heart to the next.

The Verge

The verge is what goes
from one bus stop to another.
Mostly it is daisy and weed,
though in the towns there are
scraps of rubbish, sweetie papers
and crisps which will
soon scatter in the wind.

On country verges is totemic
debris: that bottle I've watched
for a year changing to a fletch
of sea glass illuminated
by the sun, or a can of Tennent's
beaten blacksmith flat
near Auldgirth, a poem

to pain and time. The verge
sprouts trees occasionally
and thick hedge. I imagine this
to be the most ancient verge,
closest to wisdom, a verge
that opens its heart to the old
world. People should not abuse

or discount the verge: I see them
behaving terribly there. The verge
has the power to ease our most
furious longings, deposit us at the
end of our mad journeys on sweet
smelling grass, or the wet,
confusing pavement home.

The Ruins at Broomfield

The wind is hot
from some invisible continent,
and heavy,

grass heads swell,
tiny seeds and wings move
on the neck of the hills.

The slow engine of the land
is burying our scratchings,
our tousles of stones.

Andrew Donald begat
Arthur, whose wife was Emma,
and so on, and all that time

this tree grew
our words were being
grassed over and left as spoil.

Cathkin Park

In the leaf mould
and mud we suddenly
find the terracing,
so clearly defined
you'd swear
they'd just left,

the faithful,
the disconsolate.
This end of the pitch
is swallowed
by roots and trees
rattling in the wind

and to my eyes
the other end of the
pitch is swallowed by
today, its worries
and disasters as thick
as any branches.

It's all too easy,
isn't it, to
cock your ear to the
past, imagine its noises?
But we are all
in search of our daft

fathers and uncles,
the ones who might
have been there for us,
but pulled the collars
of their big coats up instead
and vanished into the mist.

The Poetry of Sparrows

I was in a beach bar,
a bit drunk, when two sparrows
sped between branches,
fretwork and the slack

jawed gaze of children,
and suddenly two lines of poetry
entered my head, lines
of unique cleverness.

Keen to photograph the birds,
I found crumbs from some
cheap pizza snack
in the bottom of my bag,

and tossed them below
my feet, then like an idiot
rubbed my fingers
into my eyes. I was blind

and weeping into the wash
of sky when I realised I had
forgotten the words:
they were not my words

anymore anyway,
but a blur of fawn
and blue and air and biscuit,
the poetry of sparrows.

Medium

An artist's medium, sandstone,
a chemical equilibrium
established over a million years
between natural fluid
and the stone's framing minerals.
Even before becoming
a work of art, it's a work of art.
Look at it raw,
imagine snapping it open
like a mould, divining
the perfect head of
a princess within, or a snake,
or an eagle ready to fly.

Important Work Interrupted

Though in receipt of a state pension, I kick
stones in strict order down the Keir Road.
The first goes into the burn, one bounce allowed,
another through the slats of the gate by the brig,

the third thrown into the scaur high enough
to miss the trees. All that accomplished,
we can sleep sound, the birds can write
on the sky, the world will not be a set

of cruel dreams but unwrap tomorrow
leish and green. Somebody came out
of their cottage the other day
and said, 'you are scuffing around weirdly

for a man your age, should you not get a dog?'
Is it not hard enough worrying about the fragile
universe with its infinite gears and cogs,
but that I should get a pet, another creature

on which to inflict empathy and pain?
I should have come out with all that there and then
standing next to that man with a face like a flat iron,
but embarrassment caught my tongue.

Hibernation

People I know are getting
confused; it's easily done,
even the weather, see:
the snow and sunshine
hammering down,

we are in a crack between,
the craic between.
'Did you know…?' someone
in the pub always asks.
Nobody knows a thing,

that's the joke. We are all
storing the same words
in our cheeks for another
year, thinking
the order matters.

My Mind

My body is falling apart
but my mind is running about
like one of those spaniels
that sees the horizon
as just a small dyke
with a rabbit behind.

I stopped trusting my mind
a long time ago, but even after
all the scrapes it hasn't
learned a thing. I have aches
in my side, but my mind
is beyond the tree line,

I have problems seeing,
but my mind is beneath
the bright shower head
of the moon. My mind
is telling me to go now
and find poetry and love:

my mind's tongue is still
lolling on the floor!
It's not right in the head,
my mind. When I'm
on my death bed,
it'll be trying all the doors.

Part v

Journey

The Pair Who Used to Play Pool
with the Pair Who Are Still Here

I'm thinking who they were, those no longer
here: that kindly northern English couple
who drove up country once a week, sipped

sherry and half pints and played, joking
in a saucy, innocent way. The pair still
here are playing pool but they are making

half the noise, having half the fun.
Life is like that, becomes through time
a re-enactment. Do you remember

that double, a red struck by error
that rocketed into the pocket, the laughter?
The shots that didn't connect. Maybe small

things endure. I'm imagining in the half-lit
space between dartboard and the drinkers'
bowed heads, they are still scoring the air.

Remembering Fine in The Imperial

It's still morning:
the hanging baskets
are moving in
a small breeze
and outside every
window a seagull rides
a grey thermal.

How refreshing to find
everyone you've ever known
but forgotten in here:
the jannie with the twisted face,
the shelpit idiot
who used to go with that nice
Geordie girl,

that man with the fishing hat
and fierce moustache.
And that enormous bloke!
How can he still
be drinking Best
when so many thin men
have fallen by the verge?

The man who was Taylor
Swift's roadie in 2011 is here.
He is a liar.
These are all miracles
worth celebrating
with a third pint,
maybe a £37 win in the puggie,

enough to stay here
and hope to see...
you know! Those ones
that were such fun
back then remember,
that did... och,
you ken fine.

Old Mo and the Ruins of Heracleion

(In memory of Ian Morrison)

I showed him the picture
but he already knew it,
her white face turned
to the light.

Mo has been in books
to their dark depths,
saw she was rooted
in Nile silt, knew her

sculptor, all this came
to him the length
of his life,
facts like fish

always brushed
his hand.
The Naiad and Mo
are in a green

light like jade.
She wears jewels
of weed. He swims
in the ruins of libraries.

Today's Funeral

Another funeral today.
Good turn out, minister
sounded like she knew him,
pies and pizza, two drinks free,
scored 4 on the funeral scale,
point off for him being younger
than me, point off for no fight.

Still not bad. Snow is turning
to sleet. The lamps outside
blur and splinter, light smears
like oil on the windows.
Everything we touch, it drains away.
He was a good man they are saying.
I wonder if he would have

traded that for six months longer
being a bad man or two years
for being downright evil?
It is a ritual of course, no one means
much of what they're saying.
He was local. Folk knew his Mum.
He had a tumour.

Things

He died in his sleep
and she was already
in a home. I watched
their things put

in a small van
and taken away:
an old bike with a bell,
a medicine ball,

a pile of *People's Friend*s,
bed frames, a guitar,
a pet carrier,
two trays, spoons,

a typewriter,
all these things and more
were gently peeled
from their cobwebs

and taken away
in steady drizzle
by a small van
along the darkening

road to Thornhill,
where, I guess,
the perfect little universe
they made, with

all its truth
and heart-stopping
intricacies
will be quietly binned.

Ghost Boats

'A squatting child full of sadness releases
A boat as fragile as a May butterfly.'
Rimbaud, 'The Drunken Boat'

The *Splendid Poison Frog,*
Spix's Macaw,
the *Bramble Cay Melomys,*
the *Moorean Tree Snail,*
the *Poo-uli,* the *Baiji,*
the *Akepa,* the *Rusty Grebe,*
all have drifted in and out of history,
and 16,000 species
are queuing in the mist
to join them.

The morning of the world
has sailed,
the afternoon and evening too.
Night brings sombre
reckonings with the
slap and pulse
of sluggish waters.
The poisoners
are our only saviours:
the last irony.

I think of the care
we have,
and the callousness.
How the next to go
extinct must be the
killers, the money
twisters, the dictators.

Then maybe the two
sides of our nature
can reconcile,

and we can tend
as we have done
at times,
for ourselves, our own,
our surroundings.
It is a long line of hope
spun in lengthening shadow
against burning clouds.
As the last boat
leaves.

Maisie Belle

I'm in Mather's today, West End,
waiting to go to some event.
Christmas crowds, the gantry
reflecting street- and lamp-light.

It's near six. It was here, in 1977,
I last saw my father. He was standing
with Uncle Jack, talking low
and urgently, unmistakably them.

I didn't interrupt,
left after finishing my pint.
I'm not thinking about
the strangeness of seeing him

then after all these years,
but the talk so hushed and important.
Was he laying it out there on the bar,
his sorrowful life? His want

to do this or that? Something
so vital he needed to bend
his bald head so close to his brother's,
like a meeting of strange monks?

The door shudders, cold breaks
like a wave. All that is mist
and breeze now, washed
over the streets and the North Sea.

The man next to me is talking
about a horse he needs to win
called Maisie Belle. In New Zealand
somewhere it is greeting the dawn.

Journey

A friend is on a journey
of remembrance or recovery.
Remembering, that's how
I'd have it, leave it

open-ended: perhaps the finale
will be a ghostly reconciliation,
the touch of shadows,
one long since, one still here

teetering on a day's brink.
Maybe not. Another friend
talks about normal people,
how they behave.

I don't know much about
them, they might have
less questions, more answers.
I bear them no grudge:

I know as days shorten
we're all going to be standing
under a throbbing ball of stars,
wondering why.

Legacy

In the Glen today
the starwort shone
on the bed of the burns
and each stone gleamed.

It was like the age
before run-offs,
pesticides and profit,
pure water ran down

the throat of the world.
At the cairn, a princess
was buried with a necklace
of Whitby jet,

the same kind I think
I bought my daughter
the day I found she was sick.
We take our love and posit

it here, below the moon
and stars. For folk
to gauge, to know we've tried
to be good as well.

North of Mendocino

Since the pain
in my leg has lessened,
I have lost the American
poets. Schwartz, O'Hara,
Myles. I don't know

why but in the tortured
early morning they were
easy with me, those folk,
charmed by trees,
run down by taxis,

hammered by lust
and hanging
their words across
the swollen sky
like torn bunting.

Now I am drinking tea
and a poet
of my acquaintance
is talking about jumping
off a ferry into

the Irish Sea:
it would be a proper
poet's death, he says.
It's better,
I reply, to walk along

the lines written for us
before dawn by the dead.

As you know
they are a moveable feast.
'Come to the table

and snatch a slice of apple.
invent a small country
just north of Mendocino
on the north-west
coast.'

3am

It is hotter than it should be:
I kick my feet out, stare
at the ceiling which, like
some dead sky, is grey,
though a car leaves now and then
a narrow wake of lemon.

Awake, it is impossible
not to wonder about others
caught in this same net,
their brains buzzing,
hoping for sleep or morning
to provide a chance to forget,

but in the meantime
lashed by the same storm.
The night brings waves
big enough to drown in,
and the shore is a smile
a hundred sweating

leagues away, a smudge
on a chart of night.
I close my eyes, see
the heads twisting like buoys
in a vast ocean, slowly
splitting our tethers.

Small Sun

I look at the photos taken
through the bus window
this morning: of course, the huge
red sun is just an orange dot now,

but there are things I didn't see:
ruts of cloud burned at the edge,
the net of trees, the rampart of hills,
and stark though those were

at break of day, they could not stop
the small sun which still sailed west,
pinned to the sky like a heart.
We must look twice at suns and folk,

their consanguinity. Here I am amidst
the litter of catheters and white plastic –
your new end of range furniture – dwarfed
by the mittened figure in the bed.

You Don't Know

'I don't know,' you shout.
The morphine line is pumping,
and you don't know.
I try and imagine
where your head is taking you,
the brick walls and panoramas,
the faces or voices dimmed
like a chorus through mist.
They say the dying thin out their dreams,
that they are peopled by the lost
but loved, landscaped in light.
It is what those at the bed-end
like to think, as outside the evening
traffic stills and rain sweeps
the pavements clear of stragglers.
But you shout, 'I don't know.'

Time to Go

Staring at my friend who is dying
I wonder: when the mirror
shows me like that

what comforts or reassurances
will I put in place?
Some sleep strategies,

a supplement,
a small procedure?
Death takes a single moment,

it is an elegance, maybe even
an unfathomable
piece of beauty.

The run-up though:
the gambling and conjecture,
the parachutes of words,

folk who really like you,
nodding, smiling, wondering
when it's time to go.

Part VI

Goodbye

Distance

This gap
between islands
twisted
with sun

isn't

it is a tune
needing notes
or
a poem needing
words
not just any

Big words
like love
desire
loss

distance

I am dazzled
by it
it is
heart achingly

cold
and beautiful
Harbours are
full stops

the sentence
between
lasts
forever.

Never Been Away

London's freezing fog
last night and then suddenly
I am crossing water and the sun
is picking out things
I've never seen: that wee lighthouse
sprouting below like a mushroom,

the straps of grey and white
on the firth. I follow the sea
like a dog off the lead,
my nose is pointed north
to where it is wild and muscled
but gleams like old gold.

The sea is like a story
so generous we have a chapter each:
there I am kicking my heels up as a boy,
skimming stones, or later
falling in love and all this
witnessed and sewn into the sea,

to its complex twists and plot lines.
Nothing could surprise
the sea you would suspect,
not the joy or sadness,
certainly not the poems,
its patience is endless.

I could not wish for a better
guide than the sea, it has been
carrying my kind for years, licking
at our feet, soothing our dreams,
meeting us after our absences
like this as if we'd never been away.

Book

I love you reading
the book I read:
the one diffused
with sunshine
and carted for years

from one summer
to the next.
Take it on trains
and boats
so I can imagine

the dawn that spills
down the pages
onto your hair
and fingers.
Take it to pubs,

parks, lochs,
wherever
there is light,
a bit of romance.
It's a story

of that, after all,
how imagined
love
writes books,
comes real.

Lux Angelis

Bright days bring spotlights
and things turn to a kind
of mind's fire:
the way you imagine
and the way you see coalesce.
These flowers finally
are salvers of sunlight

open and cupped to the sky.
I look at your face in that picture
and again it seems to me
all the component parts,
those deep eyes,
that mouth, that smile,
though wonderful are less

than the light that laces
them together:
not the sun but
the mysterious lamp of you.

Flying

All these heads above orange seats
like fruit in a crate.
Lydia says, 'what's the difference

between a mucky bus stop
and a lobster after breast surgery?'
She is 21 and studying philosophy.

Through the pill of the window,
clouds bubble, form palms and knuckles.
It is April 2023. In my book someone

has just been eaten by a shark.
There is plenty of wine left
but everyone is longing for that swamp,

the ground. The ground is overrated –
my manifesto. I say let's keep juddering
thermals between sleep and unfounded

optimism. Here where my daughters
frame a porthole of pure
blue horizon, riding our luck.

Swan

The plumage on the swan
is a dazzling white,
there
is no white whiter.
When it bends a wing
like a shield the sun
is in the cup of swan
like stars.
I know the swan is a bird
but it is also a tower,

a single shoe.
Its eyes are black
as night,
there is no black
blacker. When it curves
its neck,
you're hooked.
I know the swan is a bird
but it's also a doorway,
a question mark.

Many of the interesting
things about the swan
aren't swan at all,
they're motion and light
and tenderness.
An idea at the end
of the evening
after drinking,
warmth in the air
you can taste.

See

Walking in the woods
which are like gold
and blood,
the world is at my heels.
I sit and close my eyes
and when I open them
it is clear that there's
a fairy across
the shine of the loch
and she is infusing
the veins of leaves,
the short spans
of water with green,
she is using the fabric
of the sun
to say, look, Hugh,
I know
there are days
like these,
but see? There
are worlds within worlds.

Leaving

Through a mosaic of pink
and white rock a ferry is leaving.
It is not a calendar picture
or postcard, or the front

page of *The People's Friend*,
it is real: there is a hard breeze,
gulls are screaming, waves
muscle towards my feet.

At 3am I was in Ukraine,
at 6 talking to my daughter,
at 11 phoning the doctor,
but in the early evening I am

watching the *Lochnevis*
under a miraculous blue sky
moving slowly from my past
into the arms of the sea.

Goodbye

This dazzle stretches
away to Africa,
a long sheen like bronze
to where the sun is harder:
the wind brings light rain
fragments of other places
released by magic – petrichor –
rue and passion-flower,
eucalyptus from Algiers,

thyme from the broken
walls of Tipasa.
Dust and blossom
and ruin, the smell of poetry.
Old dazzle was tiny shards
on Loch Aline
and Arienas, up the hill
and the water lying

like a crescent moon
but, with respect and love,
farewell to these spooks.
I am older and ache
on my own accord.
I will put one thought
in front of the other,
point my nose south.

Acknowledgements

Some of these poems in this collection first appeared in *Northwords Now, Acumen, The Poetry Review, Prole, The Poets' Republic, Prairie Schooner, Bard on the Run* (Roncadora Press) and *The Opposite of Grieving* (Nine Pens Press).

Also published by **LUATH PRESS**

Not Actually Being in Dumfries
Hugh McMillan
ISBN 9781910745106 PBK £12.99

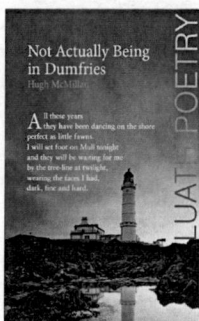

McMillan's Galloway:
A Creative Guide by an Unreliable Local
Hugh McMillan
ISBN 9781913025533 PBK £12.99

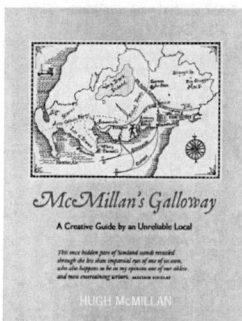

Hugh McMillan is a poet and one of Scotland's best and most unique contemporary voices. Rarely operating in the mainstream, he has yet built up a reputation for powerful, accessible and moving work, often using humour as a tool. He has been writing poetry for 30 years and this book represents the first sizeable selection of that work, along with a large number of new poems.

McMillan's imagination has a mind of its own.—THE HERALD

McMillan's Galloway takes the reader on a whimsical tour of Dumfries and Galloway through the people, places and myths of the area. Topics include the pub where Britt Ekland did not film the seductive bum scene in *The Wicker Man*, the striking similarities between fairies and little green men and the unexpected revelation of Lawrence of Arabia's tenancy in Kirkcudbright.

Although this unconventional guidebook is irreverent in tone, it's clear that McMillan's feelings for Galloway run deep. And we're sure yours will too, after joining McMillan on this witty and whimsical tour of his homeland.
—SCOTLAND MAGAZINE

Heliopolis
Hugh McMillan
ISBN 9781912147762 PBK £9.99

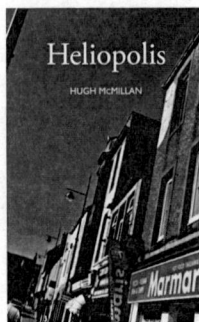

The Conversation of Sheep
Hugh McMillan
ISBN 9781912147793 PBK £8.99

Heliopolis is Hugh McMillan's sixth collection of poetry. The poems range from his kitchen table to Greece, St Petersburg and Mars. He finds the universal in the purely local and the local in the universal. Where people live, breath, hope and suffer that's where his poetry is, as legacy, dream and testament.

In a Scottish literary scene crowded with excellence, McMillan is unique in the angle and tone of his attack on the familiar.—IAN DUHIG

The Conversation of Sheep is a book by, for and about sheep. For those who live in the country sheep are strange punctuation marks in life, chewing insouciantly in the background while folk are born, work, live and die below the great and sundering sky. Some of these poems feature sheep as bucolic extras in the film of life, others delve deep into the secret nature and personalities of sheep themselves. Hugh McMillan is an award winning poet and Michael Robertson, whose photographs also populate this book, is a shepherd who lives in the same village.

Haphazardly in the Starless Night

Hugh McMillan
ISBN 9781910022894 PBK £9.99

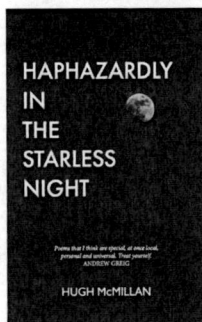

Taking in the years of the pandemic, McMillan's poetry takes us on a trip through his life and imagination, his hopes, observations and dreams.

It's never less than an interesting journey. He is an accessible, humorous and tender writer. He is one of Scotland's best.

For 25 years the teacher from Penpont has been penning verse in his individual form to some of the highest praise and it is this talent and originality that has won him countless awards.—DAILY RECORD

Whit If? Scotland's History as it Micht Hiv Bin

Hugh McMillan
ISBN 9781804251355 PBK £7.99

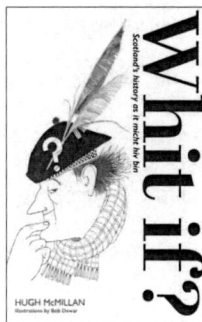

Whit if Alexander haed Twitter? Whit if John Knox haed fawen in luve wi Mary Queen o Scots? Whit if Jacques Brel haed jynt the Corries?

As both poet and long-time student and teacher of Scotland's strange and undervalued history, McMillan is the ideal guide to all the micht-hiv-bins of Scottish history, as well as all that wis. Humour is guaranteed, but that doesn't mean he won't be digging up many an educational gem along the way!

One of our ablest and most entertaining writers – pure and simple.—ALISTAIR FINDLAY

Details of these and other books published by Luath Press can be found at:
www.luath.co.uk

Luath Press Limited

committed to publishing well written books worth reading

LUATH PRESS takes its name from Robert Burns, whose little collie Luath (*Gael.*, swift or nimble) tripped up Jean Armour at a wedding and gave him the chance to speak to the woman who was to be his wife and the abiding love of his life. Burns called one of the 'Twa Dogs' Luath after Cuchullin's hunting dog in Ossian's *Fingal*. Luath Press was established in 1981 in the heart of Burns country, and is now based a few steps up the road from Burns' first lodgings on Edinburgh's Royal Mile. Luath offers you distinctive writing with a hint of unexpected pleasures.

Most bookshops in the UK, the US, Canada, Australia, New Zealand and parts of Europe, either carry our books in stock or can order them for you. To order direct from us, please send a £sterling cheque, postal order, international money order or your credit card details (number, address of cardholder and expiry date) to us at the address below. Please add post and packing as follows: UK – £1.00 per delivery address; overseas surface mail – £2.50 per delivery address; overseas airmail – £3.50 for the first book to each delivery address, plus £1.00 for each additional book by airmail to the same address. If your order is a gift, we will happily enclose your card or message at no extra charge.

Luath Press Limited
543/2 Castlehill
The Royal Mile
Edinburgh EH1 2ND
Scotland
Telephone: 0131 225 4326 (24 hours)
Email: sales@luath.co.uk
Website: www.luath.co.uk